Keelan LaForge

The Year I Stopped Running

Keelan LaForge

The Year I Stopped Running

ISBN: 9798303037755

Copyright © 2024 Keelan LaForge

All rights reserved. No part of this book may be reproduced in any form or by any electronic or mechanical means, including information storage and retrieval systems, without permission in writing from the publisher, except by reviewers, who may quote brief passages in a review

Printed in Belfast, United Kingdom.
Publisher – Independently Published

Dedication

For my mum, Pauline, who always reminds me that my value isn't in what I achieve but in the kind of person I am and how I treat others.

Chapter One

A friend of mine sent me a card reading last year. She regularly gives readings, as in, tarot readings, but I had never sought her out for that particular purpose. She told me that two cards literally jumped out of the pack for me, and she felt compelled to share them with me. They spoke to me, and it felt like they came at exactly the right moment. I'd been anxious about everything, and I desperately needed some words of reassurance. It doesn't matter how old or mature or experienced you get; you never get too old to hear the words "everything will be OK."

The first message she had for me spoke to me instantly. It was an obvious one because it referred to "peace" and knowing that everything was working out exactly as it should. The second message left me stumped for a while. It said that this was a time for purification, for cleansing the body and mind. The words themselves didn't cause me confusion, but I didn't know what their application was meant to be. Did it mean that I was unknowingly surrounding myself with toxicity? No, I decided – it wasn't anything as complex as that. There was a basic meaning behind what she'd said, and I needed to stop and reflect, in order to think of what it was. It had got lost in all the complications I'd created in my life. Sometimes you need to do some very thoughtful thinking just to find the simplest meaning in something.

I thought I'd been living a simple, tranquil life, but was I? Even though I wasn't working, I still felt overstretched and overwhelmed. Every week was a rush from Monday to Friday, and the weekend went by in what felt like a millisecond. Was I truly living how I wanted to, or was I creating chaos for myself in trying to keep up with absolutely everything? Keeping up with the commitments dished out by my kids' school felt like a full-time job in itself. Sometimes taking on anything on top of it made me feel like I was carrying more than I have the strength to support. Others might carry the same load and do it with graceful ease, but I ended up collapsing under it, and it took very little to trigger me. For as long as I can remember, I have had mental health issues, and now I know I have to keep things quiet, or I get drained to the point of breakdown at a startling rate.

Last year, we moved house and the upheaval of that was predictably stressful. I thought if we did it in small stages and in a measured way, it would barely be noticeable, but of course, it was. I don't think there's any way to make such a major life change into a smooth transition, however thinly you try to spread it out. I was ready to move, and it felt long overdue. I'd been living in an undesirable tenancy for several years. I was tired of having the walls literally falling in around us and the landlord failing to fix anything. There was a leak in the roof of our storage room and whenever it rained, the water poured in through it. There had been a carbon monoxide leak about which he had been worryingly blasé, and the wallpaper was flapping off the walls because of how damp the plaster was behind it.

Living alone with two kids in a damp house were two factors that had contributed to the pattern I'd established of constantly going out. The postman even had an in-joke with my next-door neighbour that I was never in. They took my parcels in more often than I did. Whenever the kids were at school, I focused on writing in coffee shops and cleaning up in a very rushed way, but whenever they were off, or whenever they finished school for the day, I would cram in as many activities as I could fit in. I still see so many families around us doing the exact same thing. Even though the activities I did with the girls weren't always scheduled clubs and they involved us spending valuable time together, it felt like we were always running around, afraid to miss something.

As I write this, I'm reminded of a car accident I had a few years ago. I was going to visit my sister in her town which was a bit of a distance away. I thought it might have been foolish to go that week; I just got a gut feeling about it, but I chose to ignore it because it had become our weekly ritual, and I didn't want to postpone it and let her down. The weather was getting increasingly wintery, and we had some projected snowfall, but I knew that

The Year I Stopped Running

the weather forecast was usually wrong, so I decided to go anyway. Whenever I set off, there wasn't even a skiff of snow on the ground, but after a couple of hours at her house, I looked out the window and noticed a classic Christmas scene. It was beautiful, but the last thing I wanted to do was drive in it. Still, I had to, to get home. I decided to set off before it got any deeper, but it was already dense on the ground. I hadn't seen snow like it in Northern Ireland for a decade. I set off hesitantly. There was a steep downwards drop immediately outside the cul-de-sac my sister lived in. I was driving in second gear, so I hadn't built up much speed when the car skidded, and we slid down the hill. The car spun and the back end of it hit the back of the car stopped in front of us. I was completely shaken up, and that wasn't the end of our woes for the day. We had some lovely strangers that offered to push our car back uphill since we were stuck in the snow, and they went to great lengths to do it while a group of teenagers stopped to laugh at us. I returned to my sister's housing development, got stuck in the snow again – this time without any heroes in sight. I phoned the breakdown company and told them I needed help, but before the call was finished, I managed to get the car moving again. I had to drive a long, convoluted route home, because I was too afraid to tackle the hill again. I drove so fearfully, on roads I'd never seen before, hoping they would lead me home. I got stuck in the snow again and a man ended up offering to get the car restarted for me. There were many guardian angels that appeared out of nowhere and came to our aid that day, but it was also a distressing day. I finally got home in tears, trying to hold it together for the sake of the kids. The point of this digression is to say that had I listened to my intuition and to the weather forecast, I could have spared myself all that drama. I invited it in a way, by trying to do too much. It felt like a hard lesson, but it's one I still think of today whenever I'm overloading myself with too many tasks and outings.

My mind and body always give me warning signs when I'm trying to do too much. There's multitasking, and then there's juggling to the point you're accelerating towards a breakdown. Sometimes the first leads to the second for me and I'm forced to take a step back. Sometimes when I feel most compelled to run around, that's when I need to slow down the most. Whenever I got home after that car accident, I wasn't keen to leave again any time soon. I refused to drive in even a drop of snow for a couple of years after that.

In a way, Lockdown showed me that I could, under duress, stay at home. I wasn't exactly thrilled to do it at first, but I got into a new routine and life moved at a slower pace. In a way, I was happy to cull things from my overfilled life. We didn't have the option to run here and there, or to squeeze in playdates or to attend every local community event running; there weren't any.

We did lots of valuable things together at home, just myself and my two kids. We had dance parties to my records, we baked and made crafts together. I homeschooled them for a time like every other parent. We did yoga videos together and appreciated our allowed daily walk. We got very good at filling our days with creativity and not needing to look outside our home to do it.

Whenever the museums reopened, we spent a lot of time strolling around the Ulster Folk Museum. I found it to be a great remedy for over-busyness. Most of the time we spent there, it was almost entirely deserted. We would run into the odd worker in one of the houses, cooking soda bread over the griddle and sitting in a wooden rocking chair by the fire, or hand weaving a rug, but other than that, we were faced with pure silence, apart from the crunch of our own shoes on the gravel and the sounds of my children's laughter and conversation. It was restorative. I didn't feel overstimulated, and I started to realise just how often I had felt that way. Nature suits me better than overpopulated events do.

After Lockdown ended, we fell into the habit of over-attending events again. Once you go to one, I find that it snowballs into many. You get invited to more and more and more. Even though it's lovely to have that amount of variety in your life, it's exhausting too. Sometimes you need to work out how to say no even whenever you want to say yes. It's so easy to fall into the trap of filling every minute, especially in the lead up to seasonal events. There are events for Halloween, for Christmas, for Easter, Valentine's, Mother's and Father's Day, birthdays, anniversaries, summer. The list is endless. I recently decided I needed to wisely pick and choose the events we went to, instead of

The Year I Stopped Running

trying to attend everything. Whenever you squeeze too much into a day, you end up feeling wrung out yourself. There is so much pressure in our society to always be "doing" something. Until we moved house, I did almost everything I could to avoid staying at home. But it begins to get costly – not just financially, but emotionally.

Whenever I want to get back to simplifying everything, I reflect on my childhood. I think about the things we didn't have access to in the nineties in Northern Ireland. We didn't have a host of events to attend. There was no such thing as a pumpkin patch, or a children's festival or even a coffee shop. If we went to an event, it was a rare treat. I remember going to the summer fayre at my school and spending 50p on a balloon on a spring and walking home with it, watching it bound and rebound, feeling so rich. If we went on an outing to a seaside town and got an ice cream, it felt like a real treat too. I remember going to the grocery shop in our village and getting a 10p mix in a paper bag and feeling like I'd won the lottery. The lack of options meant there was less to choose from, which in turn, made for a calmer mind and a more appreciative spirit. Whenever I talk to other mums, I see a common thread in the conversation: they bemoan the fact they haven't taken their family out enough and that they haven't done enough. There is terrible pressure nowadays to provide a full entertainment programme for your children, but it was never needed in past generations, and I think that this generation of kids is the most entitled. There's probably a link between these two factors. Why do we have to fill every moment of our lives? What is it we are worried about confronting in ourselves if we stop for a minute?

I also noticed that I was much more settled as a child at home. I was used to spending most of my time there and I had plenty of ways to counteract boredom. I'm lucky in that I have never got easily bored, but I think that is because I was allowed to be bored as a kid, and I had to find hobbies to pass the time. I have carried them into adulthood, but I notice that the busier I make myself, the less time I have left to devote to those hobbies. I start to jump from one thing to the next, never settling on one thing or getting deeply involved in it. My kids are exactly the same. Whenever we are constantly on the run, they don't know what to do with themselves at home.

I find that they pace the house, not knowing where to put themselves or what to do. They repeatedly ask me where we're going to go and what we're going to do next. Then, they tend to fight one another for entertainment and probably to get rid of the discomfort they're feeling at not knowing how to be bored.

The more we get, the less easily satisfied we are. Whenever I feel overbooked with activities, I start to appreciate each individual one less. It stops being something to look forward to and starts becoming another box to tick off on a list of our to-dos. Whenever my children get to go to lots of birthday parties, get lots of gifts from family or get a constant supply of sweets, I can see a disenchantment rising in them that wasn't there before. They seek more and more and more and nothing ever seems to satiate their appetites. I think it's the same story for adults. When we have too much, we don't know where to turn to find easy contentment. It sets us off in pursuit of that constant high, and we never grasp it for more than an ephemeral instant.

So, whenever I got that card reading, it felt serendipitous. I always analyse messages like that, believing in their meaning and their timing. I knew I needed to slow down and strip my life back to the basics. I was over-complicating everything and overfilling every moment and cluttering my mind. Whenever my mind is cluttered, my home gets very cluttered too. It's like a physical manifestation of my own mental state. Looking at it, in turn, makes me feel more stressed out and even more cluttered. I gave the card reading a lot of thought and decided that it meant I needed to remove things that were causing me stress from my sphere.

And that was how I began the journey of slowing down and savouring the smallest things instead of running in desperation after the big and often unattainable ones.

Chapter Two

So much has changed for the better in the last year. I moved in with my partner and I have experienced a level of peace and happiness I didn't know was possible. He has introduced me to ideas I never would have thought of otherwise; ideas as simple as dog-sitting. I had entertained the idea of getting a pet for years, but I always created excuses not to. I always had pets growing up and I've always loved being around animals, but I was put off by the expense and the additional responsibility. I liked being able to go away for the weekend at a moment's notice. I liked the spontaneity that comes with not being a pet-owner. I liked the fact that I don't have to worry about my pet's health, vet trips and pet insurance. I liked the freedom that comes with not being tied down by a permanent pet resident. But I never thought of dog-sitting for other people. It was my boyfriend that suggested it. He is a true dog-lover and since we didn't think we could afford to get our own dog, he decided it would be a good idea to offer to mind other people's instead.

I've never considered myself a dog person. I always liked some dogs from a safe distance, but I hadn't spent much time around them. I was a bit jumpy around them but having two dog visitors quickly changed that. They were small, curly and friendly. They followed us around the house as we did the most mundane things. I found myself filling the washing machine with a little furry friend at my feet. It was like having a toddler again, but one that didn't whine at me. I found myself brightening up around them. It's hard to be in a bad mood whenever a dog is sitting on your foot giving you its biggest smile. The kids settled down in their presence. They enjoyed helping out with walking the dogs and feeding them. They were great at keeping them entertained with games of fetch and cuddles on the sofa. It felt like it brought so much goodness into our home.

I have always loved going for long walks. I used to enjoy the morning school walk whenever my kids were in two different schools. I would use the return walk as a chance for reflection or to listen to a podcast or some music. After we moved house and the girls started going to the same school, the school walks almost vanished. (Unless you count walking to and from the car as a walk.) I was unsure about getting a dog as a pet because of the obligation to walk it every day. It's silly because I could happily walk for hours a day in all weathers, but I thought about the times whenever we were all sick. Who would walk the dog then? What if we had the flu and we couldn't leave the house for days on end? I used worries like that as reasons to resist getting a pet. The more you overthink something, the less likely you are to do it. It's the same as with writing, or any other goal. If you sit stewing in your own concerns, you don't make any headway and you stay, stuck in the same chapter forever.

After minding a couple of dogs, I started to feel the health benefits of regular walks. I couldn't make an excuse to not go, because the dogs needed to expend their energy, and I needed it as much as the dogs did. It felt like all the stagnant thoughts were lifted away with the breeze. The act of putting one foot in front of the other released something and made me feel like I was making mental progress too. People laud the benefits of tree bathing and communing with nature, and I agree that they work wonders. It felt like all the demons that had been battling away in my head all morning were dispersed with that daily walk. They went off to roam in the wilderness and didn't return to bother me.

I had phases of walking routinely, and phases whenever I hibernated and forgot the importance of it. During my walking phases, I loved to go to places that were located outside the city and where you could absorb the goodness of nature into your being. One of my favourite places to walk is the Cave Hill in Belfast. You can hike to the top of the hill in a couple of hours, or you can cheat and park at the upper carpark, walking the last twenty-minute climb to the summit. Whenever you get there, on a clear day, the view is spectacular. It helps me to put everything else into perspective. Whenever you're watching the city below you like a model town and all the little cars are

The Year I Stopped Running

rushing around like ants at work, you realise that the things that drive us in the modern world aren't that important. It's like zooming out of a small corner and seeing the huge world that exists outside of it. You realise that confined corner isn't the whole world – in fact, it isn't even a significant part of it.

Aside from the daily walks, there were so many other benefits to looking after dogs. They remind you not to take life so seriously. Watching them on a sniff trail for who knows what reminds you that huge life goals aren't that important. You can let go and just instinctively go in pursuit of the things you want and the things that make you feel happy. Getting a warm welcome whenever you arrive home involving lots of bouncing and licking reminds you of the fact that the simplest things in life are the ones that touch your heart. It's amazing developing relationships with these little creatures and seeing their emotions and the affect you have on them and that they have on you in a matter of hours. The kids brightened up when they met them and they became fast friends, and whenever the time came for the pets to go home, it was always hard to say goodbye to them. They quickly became like members of the family, and we got to know all their little quirks. Pet-sitting would never have entered my mind unless my boyfriend suggested it, but it was a gift I couldn't have foreseen. Sometimes I think about the things I have striven for in this life. There are so many dreams I have relentlessly pursued that didn't materialise, and then pet-sitting just fell into my lap. Sometimes whenever we strive for something, I think it pushes it further away. You can chase after so many things you think you're meant to be doing with your time, but then an activity presents itself without invitation and it turns out to be the best thing for you.

Feeling how naturally pet-sitting fitted in with our lives made me realise how much I have driven myself to do things that didn't. I regretted spending so much time chasing down dreams that only caused me stress. Whenever you have kids, the days can feel never-ending, but it's true that the years pass quickly. I can't believe my children are a decade old. They will never be the age they are now again, and once it's gone, you can't do anything to recoup that time with them.) I feel lucky I haven't gone out to work so I've got to watch them growing up and to be there for every important moment, but the flip side to that is that I haven't been patient through it all, and I have often been distracted – creating distractions to feed my own mind. Creativity has kept me going during the moments of monotony, but maybe it has taken precedence over everything else at times.

It's hard to strike the right balance between being healthily creative and getting lost in your imagination to the point of missing things that are right in front of you. Pet-sitting wasn't like that. it didn't distract me from family life; it enhanced it, and I loved watching my kids developing affection for the animals that visited our home.

After a while, we became pet owners rather than dog sitters. I discovered a love for pugs through hosting one in our home and I was determined to get one of my own. We got Potato less than a year after I became a self-professed dog person, and he has become like my third baby. He enriches our lives in so many ways and the things I worried about haven't materialised. We have still managed to go on a family holiday, and we found the perfect sitter for him. He has two dogs of his own that happen to get along very well with Potato. He's a social dog so he loved having their company and there wasn't an ounce of stress whenever we went away. On another occasion, it led to me finding a dog friendly hotel and bringing him with us for an overnight trip. It improved the experience in so many ways. It was a beach-adjacent hotel so Potato could run on the beach to his heart's content. He could even join us for dinner and at breakfast time he was served a bowl of his own sausages by the kind staff. It has opened a whole new world to us that I didn't realise existed. Other dog owners stop to chat to us every day and through letting Potato socialise with other dogs, it makes me much more social too. I tend to disappear into my own little world at times and it pulls me out of it and reminds me to communicate with others when I'm isolating myself without even realising that I'm doing it. I love the daily chats we have with other dog owners, and we have found so many dog-friendly events and venues. It was something I never noticed until I had a dog of my own. It's like we have been welcomed into a new world where all the dog owners become fast friends. The expense of having a dog hasn't been

The Year I Stopped Running

hugely noticeable to us because having him offsets many other costs. We tend to stay closer to home more often, taking him for walks on the neighbouring Greenway, so I don't burn through as much petrol. We don't attend many events that don't welcome dogs because we see him as a member of the family and don't enjoy excluding him from things. Any of the vet costs and other pet-related costs have been manageable to date and having our own dog has provided us with endless free entertainment.

Chapter Three

Whenever you're on the run in life, it's hard to find time to devote to anything. There have been times whenever my car has been glugging petrol and I've been running from one destination to the next. I haven't had time to process my own thoughts, and I've learnt that having time to process your thoughts is important. Whenever you don't take the time to do it, you get overwhelmed and that is whenever mental health issues abound.

Even though I don't work at a conventional job, I found myself far too busy sometimes. I ran from one appointment to the next, catching up with people and checking items off my ever-expanding to-do list. During these times, if someone were to ask me what I'd done with my week, I couldn't have told them. It all just becomes like a massive blur, and it doesn't feel like you're getting true value from any of it. It's like sprinting to and from the same point, never getting anywhere further, and not being sure who it serves. I think many of us live like this in the modern world, and even more so whenever we have bigger obligations, like work and money worries. We end up wasting our free time, living in a zombified state. We fall into the worlds in our phones and don't have the time or energy left for anything else.

During times like these, I find that the more I use my phone, the more I feel compelled to continue using it. Its effect on my attention span is catastrophic. I end up jumping from one task to the next, never really completing anything, and never finding a sense of satisfaction in anything either. I end up getting out every craft project I have and doing them in bitty ways. I stack them on the ironing board because I have nowhere else to put them, until I get completely fed up looking at them, or I'm forced to deal with them because they come down in an avalanche. Home avalanches are usually a good indicator of an overloaded schedule and mind, I find.

The Year I Stopped Running

Equally, there have been times whenever I have had to implement a phone ban and physically put my phone out of reach because its call has become too strong. It becomes like a drug, and you lose the ability to let your mind wander freely, constantly feeling drawn in by its empty allure. It interrupts every valuable activity you could fill your life with instead. I always feel heartened whenever I receive an update after such times of withdrawal notifying me that my screentime has decreased by an hour or two. Most importantly, I notice how much happier I am without it. Often, whenever I'm feeling depressed or stressed and I can't pinpoint why, it is because I've been spending far too much time on my phone. I might have thought there was something much more complex going on, but I just needed to detox from the tiny object that so controls our lives and our moods.

Whenever I decided to strip away all the excess from my life, my phone naturally fell away too. The more time I set aside for creative projects and peace, the less I felt the need to use it. It now merely exists as a practical tool that serves me when needed instead of becoming a master that I serve. It's like a religion for so many people, and it saddens me seeing hours of people's lives being drained away by social media and other unproductive phone-based pursuits. What makes me saddest of all is seeing everyone sitting on the bus, lost in their phones whenever they could be looking out the window, watching the world go by or allowing themselves time for self-reflection.

However, I also know that assumptions can't be made about how people spend time on their own phones. It's easy to jump to the conclusion that someone is mindlessly scrolling whenever they might be reading a book on the Kindle app, or writing a blog post, or sending an important email. I don't think that anyone should be judged for their phone usage, because we are all equally vulnerable to it. But I try to monitor my usage now, so I'm using it for productivity rather than time-filling. You can be too busy in person, and you can be too busy on your phone. Time ebbs away like sand through a net, and there is no way to retrieve it.

I always remember a passage in Sylvia Plath's "The Bell Jar" whenever she talks about lying in baths in all different locations, looking at the ceilings and reflecting on things. I think those moments have been stolen from us nowadays. Most people probably bring their phone into the bath with them, even though batteries and water don't mix very well. They are so tied to their phone that they can't bear leaving it behind during what should be a private moment. Whenever our hands and minds are empty, those are the times we often have epiphanies. If our fingers are tapping away and our minds are overloaded with information in those moments, there is no opportunity for creative breakthroughs or problem resolution or daydreaming. We just become slaves to our phones. We become automatons with no room for free thinking.

After a self-imposed phone detox, I noticed that I was no longer reaching for it as often. I would use it to research something I needed to know about, or to make necessary communication with family and friends, but it was no longer sucking up hours of my time for no good reason. I have always enjoyed bringing a book into the bath, but books aren't as demanding as screens. They allow you time for reflection between sentences. They don't bombard you with the fragmented pieces of stories that lead you down an informational rabbit hole, never finding anything valuable at the bottom of it. On a basic level, they don't overstimulate your brain, leaving you feeling edgy and agitated.

I notice the effects on my children of this fast-paced screen-based living, and they don't even own any devices. But they are surrounded by people that do. Their attention spans are much shorter than mine would have been as a kid. I noticed this recently whenever I put on an old movie I loved as an older child. It's filled with witty dialogue and there are moments of slapstick comedy that arrive at certain points in the film, but you have to wait for everything to build to the crescendo. You have to let the plot develop a little to get the laughs. My kids seem to be incapable of doing that. Before the beginning credits and the musical intro had even ended, they were expressing their boredom.

"Nothing's happening, Mummy."

"It hasn't properly started yet."

"When are they going to speak?"

The Year I Stopped Running

"Soon, you just have to wait a minute."

They looked at me like I had three heads.

"Can we just turn it off?"

I persevered, hoping they'd change their minds, but they just talked through it. They didn't listen to the dialogue, so they didn't hear any of the jokes. They didn't even absorb the physical comedy because they were too distracted by their own loud complaints.

"Please can we turn it off, Mummy?" they pled.

They acted like one of my favourite films was nothing but a torture device to them. It isn't their fault: everything is so fast-paced and bright and pacy these days. No one knows how to wait for a joke anymore. So, I sighed and admitted defeat. I know by now that there's no point in forcing a film on them: they're just going to talk their way through it. They won't develop a gradual appreciation for it. They won't let me hear it either, so nobody's happy.

No one knows how to wait anymore. It's the same story when we're in the dentist's waiting room and they're squirming around in their seats. Last time we went there, we had to wait ten minutes for our appointment. During that time, my daughter made a couple of trips to the water dispenser to serve herself water, went back and forth to the magazine rack, brought several magazines over for herself and her sister, failed to open them, returned them to the rack, brought over two versions of the Bible, talked about the programme that was on TV and how it didn't interest her, wriggled from her seat onto the floor, pulled herself back up, got told to sit still multiple times, asked how long it would be until our appointment started and tried to open the door that led to the dentist's room before we were called. It's like watching escaped gerbils trying to make sense of a new environment. When we get called for an appointment, they act like they've been waiting on their starting signal in an Olympic race. I don't know how to fight the pace my kids' generation moves at, and maybe it isn't always a bad thing, but slowing down and savouring the moment or waiting for the comedy to develop feels like an essential life skill. How many times will they have to endure boredom in their lives and look on it as an opportunity for patience and creativity? I think it's something we all need to learn how to do again: be happy with boredom. Otherwise, you just get lost in your phone and you're never alone with yourself. And so, you never really get to know yourself either.

I have always imposed a no screen time rule at the dinner table. Granted, my kids don't have their own screens anyway, so it would be difficult for them to fight against that rule, but I want dinner to be a time for conversation and connection. I hate seeing people in restaurants glued to their individual devices. It might buy them peace, but what's the point in going out for a family dinner if you aren't even spending time with your family while you're there?

Too much screen time robs us of our quietest moments, and we shouldn't allow it to do that. We have let a manmade creation rule our lives and rob us of our opportunities for personal breakthrough. I know I don't want to let mine do that to me anymore.

Chapter Four

I have always been an avid reader, but in recent years, it felt like I was rarely finishing a book. It's hard to see something through to the end whenever you don't have time to sit down and concentrate on it. Reading transformed from an important pastime to an empty moment filler – like scrolling through my phone but with the appearance of being something much more valuable. But how valuable is a sentence here and there if we never really settle into them? If we don't properly read and just skim and move on, it is just wasted reading time. It's the same thing as flicking between shows on TV. If you never commit to one thing and see it through, it's a waste of your time. You will never get the sense of satisfaction that comes from finishing something. You won't hold onto the story once you've closed the book for the last time. You can't appreciate something that you're only half-glancing at. With art, I believe it's useful to browse and find your area of interest. But then, you have to make time for it, or it's just sitting there, in the background like an unnoticed gift.

I have been making a point of logging the books I've been reading on Goodreads over the last couple of years. Each January, I set myself a reading challenge for the year. It isn't anything impressive: I just pick the average number of books I would like to read and set about achieving that. The act of putting books on your to-be-read list and then marking them as read and rating or reviewing them is a satisfying practice in itself. You have a concrete reference point for future reading too. It's helpful being able to remind yourself of your past reading and of the authors you've enjoyed.

There is a huge difference between reading for pleasure and reading out of a sense of obligation. There have been so many books that I didn't particularly want to read but that I felt that I "should" read, and whenever we feel like we should do something, we always do it half-heartedly. I slogged my way through Moby Dick, just to be able to say I'd completed it. But I wasn't in the right mood to appreciate it either. Maybe if I had read it whenever I felt like it, it would have left a greater impression on me. Whenever we take on a book that we aren't invested in, it ends in the story leaving us for good the moment we finish the book. There are so many stories that I have read but that haven't sunk into my skin, burrowing their way into my character the way the books I love do. I used to do so many things because I felt like I "should" do them instead of because I felt any inclination to do them. If you force yourself into reading for the wrong reasons, you will make yourself resent doing it and it will lead to the opposite effect you intended as a reader.

So, I stopped putting pressure on myself to read the canon this year and I looked for books that aroused my interest instead. I felt drawn to crime, mysteries and non-fiction books that covered topics like housekeeping, budgeting and enjoying the simple things in life. I wanted to read books with an immediate hook, whether it was due to great storytelling, a powerful plot or just a relevance to my own life. Releasing myself from the need to read certain books actually made me read much more. Instead of reading a few pages and then leaving a book ignored in the corner until I eventually retired it to the bookcase or returned it, unread, to the library, I was tearing through topics I really wanted to learn about. I was allowing myself to consider reading to be a valuable use of time again. The guilt I had felt over reading the same page repeatedly, never taking it in and neglecting other tasks to do it was gone. I felt the joy of reading returning to me. It reminded me of reading as a kid. I could appreciate high literature, and still enjoy the quick twists of Agatha Christie or the conversational style household tips of Kate Singh. It didn't mean I didn't have the mental capacity for more, but maybe in this stage of life, reading was supposed to be fun escapism and a useful tool in my homemaking, rather than something intellectually stimulating worthy of university level essay analysis.

I wanted to read books that evoked the seasons. In Autumn, I wanted to read cosy mysteries and practical guides with tips I could implement in my own

The Year I Stopped Running

life. I wanted to lie on the sofa, snug with a book and forget about whatever might be worrying me in the current moment. It was easier to commit to light reading in that phase of life. I knew it mightn't always be the case, but I needed reading that fitted around my lifestyle; not reading I was trying and failing to squeeze in.

We often set rules for ourselves without even realising that we are doing it. One of mine was that I could only read one book at a time and commit to finishing it. I let that rule slide and started to read more than one book at a time: different books for different moods and different settings. A paperback or hardback on the sofa in the evening, a library audiobook during the day when I had chores to do. The joy in reading became more about the immersion in the experience than about the final outcome: ie: completing a to-be-read tick list.

I'd always loved to read in the bath, even though it usually resulted in dogeared, damp books and soggy magazine pages that never returned to their original shape when dry. That was how I wanted to practise the activities that I enjoyed: to wholeheartedly immerse myself in them without worrying about the imperfection that came from the practice.

I have always been loath to borrow books from people because I worry about the state they'll be in whenever I return them to the original owner. Some people care greatly about the condition of the book, but that doesn't bother me. As my mum says, she likes to see someone really read a book: to see them bend the pages back and get engrossed in it rather than peeking between the barely fanned pages so they don't spoil the look of the cover.

This year, I've realised how long it had been since I'd made time to relax in the bath. It used to be something I did regularly. It was an activity that got me through the early years of motherhood, but I'd forgotten to make time for it. At one time, I had a bath tray with a slot for a wine glass, a candle holder and a rack for my kindle, but I'd sold it because I didn't "have time" to use it. That was the problem: I didn't have time to do things, but I could have found the time if I just rejigged a few things. When you spend your life running around, it can be easier to jump in and out of the shower, and showering can be an enjoyable experience too, but not whenever it's so rushed you barely feel the water touching your skin.

I made a point to have a bath and to read *The Simple Things* magazine in it. I only had about half an hour, but I decided to use the time wisely instead of using it to dry dishes or put away laundry, or another task that will always be there waiting for me to do it. There are times whenever I can enjoy the meditative state I go into when carrying out these tasks, but it wasn't the day for them. I always find that whenever I make time for the things that I need to do for my mental health, everything else falls into a new configuration and I always get it done in the end anyway, just as it always inevitably crops up again. Being a stay-at-home mum isn't a job that's ever finished. There is never a lull, so you just have to make your own where you can, or whenever you need them most.

So, I've been making time to read again. Sometimes we get so goal-oriented and driven in the society we live in that we start to see projects without clear end goals as a waste of time – but that doesn't mean that they are. If you think of the days before our phone usage blasted through the Earth's atmosphere, people made time for pastimes other than scrolling. They read, knitted or baked. They did needlework and tasks that required time and focus. But it was never viewed as wasted time in those days.

I have a tendency, like many people nowadays, to think that if something I do doesn't yield great results, it wasn't worth wasting time on it. But you always learn something from the moments in which you make a mess, or things don't go to plan. For example, if you a read a book you didn't enjoy, but you saw it through to the end anyway, you will have taken some sort of lesson from it – even if it was only narrowing down the categories of books you truly want to read. Whenever you're a writer, reading informs your writing - even bad reading. If you do a cross-stitch sample and it ends up looking like a tangle of thread, at least it is a starting point: either you grow from there or you give up and pursue something else you enjoy instead. You might learn it just isn't for you, but at least you tried and eliminated something to make room for something else. Nothing is a waste of time – apart from

The Year I Stopped Running

intentionally wasting time, scrolling and distracting yourself from all the things you could be doing instead.

I believe that there is a voice inside us that quietly (and sometimes loudly) tells us what we are meant to be doing and if we are on the right path. Mine is very insistent. Whenever I listen, it helps me to scrap the things that aren't serving me and to pursue the things that are. The more you familiarise yourself with it, the easier it gets to decide what to do with your time. It's only whenever I fall into making myself overly busy that I struggle to hear its advice.

So, this year, I decided to set aside more time for the things that could be called "time-wasting." Napping is another one of those things. It's something I have often fought doing because it feels like it eats up hours of the day that you could have been spending in more profitable ways. But if your body is telling you to rest, it's usually for a good reason. Whenever I fight the urge to rest, it usually results in sickness or exhaustion. You end up paying for it later whenever you deprive yourself of it. I always viewed napping as a lazy practice, and one that takes away from all the other household and creative tasks you could be doing instead. But then I realised that it's needed sometimes and whenever you submit to sleep, it often improves your productivity afterwards. If you're in a zombified state and trying to write a book, nothing but drivel will come out. There have been sentences I have composed in that state that later perplex the editor in me that tries to finetune my books. After a rest, I often home in on a phrase that's straight to the point when I might have pussyfooted around the point for an age otherwise, never quite making myself understood to the reader.
There's no such thing as time wasted in doing the things your body needs to do and the things that enrich your life without profit or trophy-worthy acclaim.

I have written myself to death at times. I remember sitting in a coffee shop once and I was writing a book but was far too exhausted to focus. I fell asleep for a minute sitting up writing and I only came around because I heard a stranger commenting on it. I realised that no good writing was going to come out of that, and I had to stop driving myself so much. If you aren't enjoying the process, it shows in your writing. After all, who wants to read a book written by a sleeping author?!

Chapter Five

Being happy at home has been something I have immensely struggled with over the years. I'm naturally a restless sort of person. I probably could have happily lived on the road, moving from place to place and having new adventures each day. My dad used to joke that I should just live in a caravan. It's hard to fight against the grain of what makes you function as a person. You must keep filing away at it and it only starts to take shape after a long period of intensive practice. I kept moving from one house to the next, even whenever I stopped having to. Circumstances in my life meant that I kept setting up house in a new place, before deciding I needed to relocate again. It was tiring, taking apart the homes I'd worked hard to put together, but that ultimately felt unhomely to me, however cosy I made them. It felt like I had an unhealthy addiction to moving house. I was hiring a moving lorry each year or constantly doing multiple car-runs to move our possessions to a new location.

I used to spend all my time at home whenever I was married, and to my detriment. I was constantly scrimping and saving, watching TV and having a one-sided conversation with my baby. She couldn't respond yet, but her smiles assured me my conversation wasn't boring her. I was enslaved in my home, and I didn't have the personal choice to come and go as I pleased, even if it was for a walk. It always felt like I'd have hell to pay later. Some people experience trauma, and they go inward to deal with it; I went outward and tried to redirect my focus into other things instead. I developed an aversion to being at home. I dreaded returning there. I had my kids, but they weren't a substitute at the time for adult company. I would have done anything to avoid going home to the empty, quiet rooms that housed our possessions. It was the most active kind of avoidance: I was running around to get away from myself and from having to face depressing fact that my marriage had failed and that I was alone as a parent.

Even as the years progressed, I kept up the habit of going out. I found a house I was able to settle in for a few years, but there were constant problems with the building. It was over a hundred years old, poorly maintained and very damp. The longer I spent in it, the more depressed I became, because I was looking at all the mess and I knew I could do nothing about it. It wasn't my place; it was my landlord's, and he was unwilling to make the slightest improvement to the place. He'd come over now and again, whenever I told him that something had stopped working. At one point, there was a gas leak from the boiler, the alarm sounded on and off and he told me it was just a fault with the alarm. A day or two later, it turned out it was a true gas leak, and he had the old boiler pulled out and another second hand one - probably circa the same year as the original one - shoved in. I would obsess over such details whenever I spent too much time at home. I would look around and see all the grime I hadn't had time to get to – or that I simply couldn't cure with some good old-fashioned scrubbing. The place needed an entire overhaul that it wasn't going to get. I kept hoping that things would turn around; that I'd draw some goodness out of my landlord, through years of regular rent payments and respectful treatment of his house, but no – people that are tight with money and lazy with repairs aren't motivated by things like that. They do everything in their own good time, ie: never.

I started to take out memberships at places that I could take the kids to. We joined the National Trust, the museums in Northern Ireland, Castle Espie wetlands centre, Funky Monkeys soft play, and anywhere else that provided subscription services that worked out cheaper when you paid annually or monthly, rather than per visit. We spent our days in nature, healing and avoiding our home. Whenever it neared the end of the day, I always felt disappointed to go home. I knew the stench of dampness would hit us as soon as we walked in the front door. It had even carried into the interior of my car. No air freshener disguised the smell, and I was sure other people

The Year I Stopped Running

could smell it off my clothes. It made me paranoid, and I wanted to avoid those uncomfortable feelings as much as possible.

The girls and I began to run around at a pace I could not keep up with. It always seemed to end in illness. We'd be skipping around the country, going to every possible event, packing our days with items of interest, but one of us would always end up falling sick, or the chores were left undone at home as we passed through, like people transferring to their connective train journey. We were there in body, but we weren't in spirit – and we were barely there in body either.

Whenever I found out we were moving house, I resolved to spend more time at home. I didn't want another running joke to come up between our new neighbours and the postman about me never being at home. I wanted to actually live in the place we called home. There are times of the year whenever perpetual movement becomes uncomfortable, particularly in the Wintertime, around the approach to Christmas. The streets are chockful of traffic and angry drivers, every public place is packed, and germs abound. Almost every time we start going to every community-run event going, we come down with the flu, or tonsilitis or an ear infection. It's like a physical representation of what we are doing to ourselves, and I think much of society lives in the same way.

I've noticed that as Christmas gets closer, there are more and more cars on the road: the volume that would have come out on Christmas Eve in the past for their final Christmas shopping trip now make an appearance from early November. Between Halloween and Christmas and all the prebooked activities, we are living in a new kind of chaos. I don't want to spend my life in the car, driving around, often aimlessly, looking for somewhere to go to.

I started to dream about my new house. I didn't do much in terms of searching for one. I just waited for the right listings to find me. I had been to what felt like a million viewings to no avail. In my mind's eye, I could already see the house I wanted to live in, but I didn't know if it was possible on my budget. I knew I wanted huge, almost panoramic windows that overlooked a garden. I wanted more outdoor space for my kids to play and for me to sit outside and join them at the wooden table we owned, reading and listening to them playing without sitting right in the middle of their ball game, ducking each time the ball flew past. I wanted a garden where I didn't have to retract the washing line every time they wanted to play outside. I wanted a space in which I didn't have to constantly play referee because we were all on top of each other all the time. Some part of me denied myself my fantasy, because I felt like I didn't deserve it. I'd put up with years of mistreatment from landlords and agencies. They happily took my money each month and left me in conditions akin to squalor. But I kept imagining something better and it did come. The first time I walked into the house I'm sitting in now; I knew it was the right one. It had huge windows that let in vast quantities of light. I could imagine myself writing there and daydreaming out the window. I think if you can picture yourself somewhere without having ever entered it before, it's a good sign that you're meant to be there.

Before I walked into the house, it wasn't the most obvious choice to me. I'd got used to being very central to everything. I could basically fall out of bed and roll into a coffee shop. The kids' school was on our doorstep. It felt like we were in the right location, but in the wrong house. The house would never be in the state I wished it was in. Whenever we cleared all the furniture out of the house and my mum was helping to clean my room, she said if someone had told her she'd walked into a Victorian hovel, she would have believed them.

Moving further away from everything has changed things. I do miss being in the middle of the city buzz. It's much quieter here. You barely hear traffic, or anything. The houses are well spaced out, but it feels like you can breathe. The air feels fresher. I can see the night sky now. That's another benefit of living here that I couldn't have foreseen: being able to stargaze. I used to love looking at the night sky when I used to smoke. It felt like a private moment of communion between myself and the universe. But after I quit smoking, I stopped standing outside at night and I started to miss those moments of stillness.

In our last house, I could never see the stars or the moon. There were too many houses packed closely together so you didn't have a hope of seeing

The Year I Stopped Running

anything over the rooftops. Maybe there was too much artificial light too. But whenever I took one of the dogs we were looking after out to the garden in the new house, I noticed the twinkly expanse of sky. I'd never noticed it before, but we were in the optimal position for stargazing. I could see all the constellations spread across the sky and I loved staring at them. Whenever Venus made its appearance beside the moon last week, it felt like we had front row seats. Had I never moved house and had I never started dog-sitting, I never would have noticed the lights in the evening sky. I realised we were on a flight path too and I enjoyed watching the planes coming and going, making up stories about where the passengers were going and what they were doing in that moment for my own entertainment. There was a super moon recently and it felt like it was so close we could reach out and touch it with our fingertips. It looked so much more impressive and imposing in a truly dark night sky.

Another moment that made me realise the benefits of our new life was whenever my boyfriend started his current job. I drive and he doesn't, so I offered to drive him to and from work. It's only about a ten-minute drive, but it's in the middle of the countryside, located in a place with no streetlights and poor visibility for walkers. There aren't any footpaths on most of the roads. Whenever he told me he was working the 7am shift, the non-morning person in me internally groaned. I didn't want to have to get up and ready at that early hour and drive before my eyes had fully opened, but I wanted to take him to work so he didn't have to walk. On one of the first drives, when I expected to feel depressed by the entire situation, I realised the beauty we got to see in the sky. It felt like we were some of the first spectators of the sunrise. There is a part of the drive where you reach a point on a hill that gives you a far-reaching view of the sealine. At that time of the day, we get to see the sun rising over the sea. The colours in the sky would make any artist and their paintbrush jealous of nature's palette. It's something we would have missed had we not ended up doing that simple daily practice. I always return home feeling refreshed rather than drained. There's something to be said for rising early. Even though I'm a self-proclaimed night owl and a reluctant early riser, I notice my mood improving the earlier I get up. It makes me more productive, but not in a pressured way. I come home feeling inspired by the sight that started our day off. I want to do creative things on the back of that feeling.

Taking time to look up at the sky sounds like such a simple thing. It's right above us every day, and yet, I didn't notice it for years. I used to walk around as if I had my own personal grey cloud suspended above my head. I looked at the footpath more often than I ever looked up. I always remember a Christian phrase I heard in a church once (and I'm not religious.) "Don't forget to look up." There are so many ways to interpret that phrase. I think in the context of the church, they were referring to turning to God, but I interpret it differently. I think whenever we get too busy, it can be easy to forget to pause and look at the sky, but it's important to do it. It puts everything into perspective and reminds us of what is truly important. I make a point of doing it now. I sit and type in front of the window and watch the activity in the sky. Sometimes it's the slight movement of a cloud, the appearance of a rainbow, or just noticing the arrival of a variety of birds that have come to eat the fat balls I've provided in the bird feeder. In my last house, no matter what I did, I couldn't draw birds to our garden. Maybe there were too many predatorial cats living locally, but they just didn't set foot on our property. I tried to lure them in with different treats and a homemade bird bath, but nothing drew them there. Whenever we moved here, I noticed whenever I put food outside, it drew more than one kind of bird. Yesterday, I noticed a robin, a blackbird, a crow, a blue tit and some starlings all feasting on the fat balls. Slowing down and spending more time at home has allowed me to remember the little things, like refilling the fat ball feeder. It might seem like a small, insignificant thing, but it isn't. It's part of the whole patchwork of experiences that give us satisfaction.

After having recent thoughts about remembering to gaze into the sky, or at least, glance upwards, I came across an article in a magazine I was reading. It comprised several photos taken of the sky and an accompanying piece lauding the benefits of stargazing and cloud watching. Sometimes it feels like everything in life neatly ties together, like a present so neatly packaged I could never have wrapped it myself.

The Year I Stopped Running

Chapter Six

As an empath, I have always been easily drained by interactions with others and the energies surrounding me. I absorb other people's energies, whether positive or negative. I have to be careful about what I take on because I get very easily overwhelmed. Working out how to have appropriate boundaries surrounding that has taken a lot of time and trial and error. I gain energy by being in my own company, creating and writing and reflecting on things. That is how I regain the energy to share with others. I think that's just a natural part of being an introvert. My daughter seems to be the complete opposite to me: she gains energy by being sociable and talking to as many people as she possibly can, preferably all at once.

In the past, I made myself overly busy, just to avoid spending time with myself. In those quieter moments, I would have unwanted and uncomfortable thoughts that I didn't want to face up to. It was easier to just keep myself distracted with constant external noise and activity. I would book every available activity I could. Over the holidays, for example, I would take the kids to every Christmas activity we could afford to do. We would go to a grotto, screenings of Christmas movies in packed cinemas, festive markets, crafting sessions, community programmes, music events, cultural events, themed visits to museums and fairs. Every season was packed with an events programme that was inspiring, enriching and exhausting. I'd usually end up burning out and getting sick, and that would be the end of it. Once we even got sick on Christmas Eve, so after all the anticipation and build-up to Christmas, it was spent as a pyjama day, and I was unable to touch the Christmas dinner I'd still felt obliged to prepare. I've never been great at doing anything in a measured way. I'm either there every minute or absent for months. It's something I recognise in myself, but whenever I'm

The Year I Stopped Running

experiencing a phase of increased energy, I find it hard to pace myself. I have bipolar disorder, and I've always had those cycles of sky-high energy juxtaposed with basement level lows.

Whenever we moved house, we had less money. Things were tight over the Summer months and into the Autumn. Our financial situation had changed, and we had to wait for everything to find equilibrium again. That meant that we didn't have the same options that we'd had before. We were never rich, but we'd had disposable income before. Now, we couldn't take out any new memberships. I watched memberships expiring, realising that I hadn't made full use of them recently. Sometimes I wanted to, but sometimes it was just too much effort, and I didn't have the energy to make the journey there. Living in the new house was consuming my time. We had bigger gardens to attend to and I was learning how to do tasks I hadn't had to do before, like strimming and cutting the grass. The place looked pleasant whenever we arrived, so I wanted to keep it that way. It had always felt like a waste of time doing deep cleaning in our last house because no matter what you did, it never looked any better. It was like trying to polish a stone in the hopes that it would turn into a gemstone if you scrubbed hard enough. Even feverish scrubbing didn't result in the house looking any brighter; it was lacklustre even after the heartiest cleaning session. In the new house, it was in good condition when we first saw it. We didn't have to do any deep cleaning at the beginning, but I wanted to keep it looking as good as possible. I felt motivated to put time and effort into my house because it was giving me gifts in return too.

I used to be much more of a homebody before having children. Maybe it's a natural result of having children; they have so much energy and I find you have to take them out to burn it off. Mine have always been particularly energetic when they you don't run it off. I've never understood how some parents manage to live peacefully with their children without setting foot outside the house. But our new house ended up being ideally positioned for other walkable spots. I mightn't be able to quickly walk to my nearest favourite coffee shop, but we were a stone's throw from our favourite library, right beside the Greenway (a walkway that feels like a little forest) for walking amidst the trees, and in late summer, the blackberries, and we are sandwiched between a couple of great parks. We started to venture less far from the house when we started dog-sitting. We took the dogs on a couple of daily walks, either in the local area or to a park a few blocks away. It felt good burning less petrol on days out. We might use more to do the school run now, but I find us staying more local on weekends. With my boyfriend's job, we need to be closer to home so he can get to and from work anyway. It leads you to uncovering the items of interest in your locality instead of always searching for something further afield.

I started crocheting this year. I'm still in the early stages of it. I've made a couple of hats and scarves and a few granny squares. But I'm enjoying the relaxation I've come upon in the practice. I discovered that a local newsagent conveniently sells yarn at a much cheaper price than any of the bigger name stores. I would never have thought to set foot there before we moved, never mind expected to find wool there. It's like a sewing shop at the back of the store, which is good to see because it feels like independent craft stores are a dying breed. I've wanted to crochet for years, and I've made a few limp attempts at learning it, but I never found the time to do it properly until this year. I was motivated because I wanted to learn how to do a single stitch, and to then build upon that gradually, with no pressure applied. Whenever I wanted to conquer the craft in a day, it never felt achievable. I'd get frustrated with myself after a few minutes because I couldn't craft the crocheted items that other people have spent decades mastering. I wanted immediate results in the same way I complain that my kids do. When I took it a little bit at a time and set myself smaller goals, or none at all, they suddenly became much more achievable.

I find sitting down and doing a quiet activity like this at the end of the day reenergises me. After a day filled with childcare, housework, writing, cooking, errand running, etc, it is nice to do something that requires no verbal or literary effort. Once I get the hang of the stitch, I can daydream while I do it. Keeping my hands busy while my mind relaxes has always been infinitely more relaxing to me than sitting still with nothing to do.

The Year I Stopped Running

I think there is a definite connection between our mental and physical health. Maybe I'm just more attuned to it because I have to closely manage my mental health all the time. The slightest thing can set me off, and I can't always predict what that thing will be. The more I tire myself out physically, the faster a mental breakdown comes. There are seasons whenever I get overloaded, and that is usually what precipitates the sickness. You can do all the running around and people pleasing you like, but I learned a couple of years ago that whenever you spend Christmas day too sick to contemplate eating Christmas dinner, it doesn't feel like it was all worth it in the end.

Sometimes it feels like it isn't possible to pace ourselves, and I still have a lot of work to do in that area. I tend to take on far too much one minute and then I crumble under the pressure the next, even if that pressure is only caused by several baking projects I've attempted to take on in one go. I find it very difficult to focus on one task at a time. My boyfriend was laughing at me recently because he said I'm always multitasking. I'd been making a point to just read on the sofa in the evening, without embarking on anything else at the same time, but he turned to me as I read my paperback, my kindle cushioned in my lap. "Are you reading two books at once?" he asked, laughing. I was, and I hadn't even realised I was doing it until he pointed it out. Maybe some of us are just wired to do more than one thing at a time. That, in itself, isn't a negative thing, but it's important to notice when you're doing it to your own detriment.

I can remember myself doing that even whenever I was in school. In secondary school, I went to a school more than ten miles from where I lived, so I had to get the bus to and from school every day. Annoyingly, our school bus didn't depart school until forty-five minutes after the school day ended, so we found ourselves hanging around, killing time, feeling the weight of the load of homework that awaited us whenever we finally did get home. During that time, I was taking guitar lessons in school, so I had to cart my guitar case back and forth – nothing, I know, compared with a cello or a tuba, but it still felt like a lot, especially with an art folder, a hockey stick, a PE kit, a schoolbag and whatever else we were required to bring in tow. I decided, as well as my guitar lessons during the school day, that I wanted to be in the school orchestra. I was already in the choir, which took up an afterschool afternoon each week. On top of that, I decided to join the drama club. I was getting piano lessons at the time too, also during school hours and sitting music exams. We were getting a lot of homework by then, compared with what we'd had in primary school. I was trying to socialise at the same time; spending weekends at friends' houses and having sleepovers. It felt like I never stopped, but I had the energy for it. It didn't feel like a huge burden, but it didn't occur to me that I could have pared things back a bit. The orchestra was a waste of time. The music teacher didn't know how to incorporate the two guitarists into the rest of the orchestral arrangements, so we were closed away in a side room like a bad smell and handed sheet music for the *Eastenders* theme tune to learn by ourselves. I didn't realise at the time that it was just her way of just getting rid of us, but had I known that I might have thought twice about staying an extra hour after school to be "in the orchestra."

There are so many commitments we take on that others aren't as committed to as we are, and they drain our time and energy. I think it's important to regularly assess what we really need to do and what we are getting from each experience. Even if it's just the joy of helping someone, that's a good reason, but if we don't know what we are getting but it is just draining for us, maybe it's time to cut a few of the things from the calendar.

Since having children, I find December to be the busiest month. In the run up to Christmas, there are so many activities packed in. On the day I write this, the kids have a festive run in school, which doesn't affect my routine, but there are items to be sent in for it. Albeit it's just a Christmas hairband and an extra pair of socks, but it's something else to remember, something else to pencil into the calendar. Each day, there is a new activity. I had to send in a five-part costume for my daughter's nativity last Christmas. Luckily, it comprised pieces that we mostly already had lying around, but in the past, I probably would have stressed myself out over it, running around shops trying to find the right items. Last year, I just used what we already had, I ordered a T-shirt online and we picked up a Christmas garland at a craft fair that could be used as a tinsel halo. In previous years, I can remember running around,

The Year I Stopped Running

taking part in charity collections, buying Christmas presents for everyone we knew, going to every community event running, whether I felt like it or not. I remember years of pushing sickness away, telling myself I was OK and to keep running at the same pace, just in time to be floored as soon as the holidays started. The holidays are supposed to be enjoyable and restful. They aren't supposed to merely be for recuperation from whatever illness we have brought upon ourselves by pushing ourselves too hard. It feels unfair arriving at our reward for all our hard work too exhausted and ill to appreciate it.

I want to carve out time for quiet this year. I have been prioritising the things I often come up with excuses not to do – not because I don't want to do them, but because they don't feel like the most productive use of my time. When my magazine subscription to The Simple Things arrives, I often open it and set it aside in a box file for whenever I finally have time to read it. And then I never do. I pick a couple of bits out of it – a cake recipe, inspiration for my painting, a quick peruse over the "My Day in Cups of Tea" article. But I rarely make time to really read it. On the envelope, quite appropriately, the words "if you're too busy to read this magazine, you need to read this magazine" are printed. It's a great reminder to me to set aside time to intentionally read my magazine. I can forget about time and place whenever I'm doing it. If I need to be pulled back to reality to fulfil one of my obligations, I set an alarm on my phone, and then forget about it until it sounds. It might seem like an unproductive use of time, but I always feel great after it, and more energetic – ready to tackle whatever I have to do after it. Time has taught me that being quietly alone energises me. Skipping rest is like running on a dangerously low battery; you can't make anything else work if you haven't set aside the time for yourself to recharge.

There have been so many magazine subscriptions of mine that have ended up being passed on, almost unread, to my family. It's strange because I get so excited about the arrival of the magazine, but then I don't find the time to read it. It's like a child getting a new toy and losing interest before they've managed to even get it out of the box because there are too many other distractions around. It's sad whenever you think about how diminished our attention spans have become in recent years. I know I'm not the only one that has this problem. It's just easier to scroll through already formed ideas than it is to do the work of finding your own. We've all got so used to reading on screen all day long too. But for me, reading online doesn't have the same impact. It just feels like it's lacking something: the paper pages. Whenever you're reading online, you have no sense of where you are in the book or article. You just know you're on a new page, but it could easily have all been printed onto one page and we mightn't have even noticed. The text is all compacted together, so it fits on the smallest screen. The romance of reading has been lost. That was the reason I resisted getting a kindle whenever my friends first had one. I didn't want to lose the slow enjoyment of reading – the activity that marries the brain to the hands. It is your hands turn the pages and allow your eyes to do the reading.

I have since discovered that Kindles have their uses, namely whenever you want to travel without carting an entire library around with you and whenever you're eating, and you don't have free hands to turn the pages. I once tried to use a book stand my mum had purchased before the days of Kindles, and that was hilariously unsuccessful. The book kept flopping forwards off the stand, and I couldn't get the bookmark to hold the pages ajar enough to allow me to read the words inside. But my heart still belongs to real books. I love the social side of reading real books too: you can pass them on to friends and family whenever you're finished, you can go in person to the library, make real connections with the staff and other readers there and read the same copies that they have already enjoyed. I'm sure there is a way to share Kindle books with friends once you've finished them, but I still haven't figured it out. There's nothing that beats the simplicity of holding a book in your hand and then passing it into someone else's. It's like the difference between real connections and virtual ones. The virtual ones can mirror real connections, but they will never be as solid as them. There is always a distance in virtual communication that there isn't in being present with someone in body and voice.

I began to go to the library on a weekly basis. It's a two-minute walk from our house and my kids love the ritual as much as I do. We go so often that whenever we miss a day, the staff remark on the fact we weren't there the

The Year I Stopped Running

previous week. I love the smell of used books. I love the fact that I can borrow hardback books with ribbon bookmarks inbuilt – books I would never feel I could justify spending money on. On the rare occasion I buy a new book, I always opt for the paperback, or the kindle version – whichever is more budget friendly. It just feels too extravagant, spending upwards of twenty pounds on a copy of a book that I might finish for good in a twenty-four-hour period. Worse, I'm worried I won't enjoy it and won't finish it. I used to see every story through to the end, whether I was enjoying it or not, but now I leave books unfinished as often as I finish them. If the story doesn't engage me, I don't want to waste my precious reading time on it. There is always a better book to read, and I don't want to make myself suffer through it for no reason other than being able to tick "finished" on Goodreads.

Recently, I haven't been reading as much and I am trying to go with the flow of that. It disappoints me whenever I lose the ability to read prolifically, but I think it's just part of my mental health condition and it's a natural ebb in life. Sometimes I am engrossed by stories, and other times, I can barely bring myself to finish a paragraph. It is just a time for a different interest. Whenever I don't want to read and write, I often find that I want to cook and clean. I often wonder how many people can keep up with the things they love consistently. Is chopping and changing just a part of the human condition, or is just part of mine? Either way, it's valid and it's a fact of life. There is no point in fighting the tide too strongly. Whenever I do that where reading is concerned, I end up reading the same page over and over again, never getting any further with the story.

In many ways, reading over the years has saved me from more frivolous pursuits. If I think of the time I devoted to reading at university, it prevented me going out all the time, spending every penny I had. I have always loved shopping, and I adore clothing. If I didn't have other outlets like reading and writing, I would probably bankrupt by now.

There was a phase this year when I was reading book after book from the library. Reading comes in waves like that for me. I think I have always carried a terrible burden with me of feeling I have to continuously be productive. Maybe it came from school and the constant workload and all the activities I packed into my days. Maybe it's from being able to watch what other people are achieving through social media; it naturally makes you feel like you aren't doing enough or that you aren't enough, full stop. We live in a particularly competitive and individualistic time. People care more about making themselves into a successful brand than they do about their community. I can't help admiring people that lived through the World Wars because they were taught to prioritise caring for others over promoting themselves. The world of self-promotion is exhausting, and it has never been something I have taken to. Perhaps that is why my pursuits have never amassed a great following: I don't want to spend, or rather, waste time on self-promotion over the other things I could be doing. It looks empty to me, even if it pays off in terms of profit. I'd rather do the smaller, more fulfilling and traditional things that have made people happy throughout history. Filling time without accounting for how you've spent every minute through your productivity is something that used to be an acceptable pastime; it doesn't feel like it is anymore. That saddens me, but it also makes me want to fight against it. In Esther Emery's "What Falls from the Sky", she demonstrates what happens to herself and her family whenever she strips everything back to basics and filters out the distracting noise that comes with over-connectivity to the internet and the pursuit of constant productivity.

I often find that ideas and important thoughts are stifled by the noise of our world. You can get so wrapped up in achieving and doing that you forget to be in a passive state, to receive gifts and messages from your own mind. With heads crammed with so much information, it feels inevitable that our systems will crash sooner or later. Whenever I read a paperback book, I find ideas swelling in my mind. It gives you more time to sit and ponder things. The physical act of turning the paper page feels like progress in itself. Whenever I'm feeling unable to read, I want to allow the silence to be heard. I think so many of us fear silence now, because we might be forced to address things about our lives that we don't want to consider and that we don't want to change. But there's something much truer about silence than there is about the constant bombardment of information from our society.

The Year I Stopped Running

I think the more we get back to interests that engage our brains and our hands, the simpler life becomes. Even for people that aren't natural readers, there are so many alternatives with which we can fill our time. For example, I was at a fair at a National Trust estate a few years ago and I distinctly remember a guy selling his own woodwork. He had made so many pieces of furniture. Building and DIY isn't a topic that interests me, but I can appreciate the work that goes into it and the skill involved. Maybe someone with more of a practical mindset would thrive with a hobby like that.

The reciprocity between the hands and our brains gives us a feeling of communion with ourselves, and I don't mean that in the religious sense. It just feels like we are working in coordination with our truest selves. It quietens the inner noise that plagues us the rest of the time. It's a busy time to be alive and it's imperative for our own wellbeing that we set aside time to devote to simpler practices.

Even at home, I have often found that I make myself laden with too many tasks to ever achieve anything. I start projects, expecting myself to complete all of them, but there are only so many hours in the day. We each have an allotted amount of time, and we have to prioritise the things we want to do. I sometimes find that I have aspirations to be a certain person, but I can't be all of them at once. For example, I want to be an seamstress, a crocheter, a painter, a writer, a reader, a cook, a parent, a cross-stitcher, an embroiderer, a quilter. I want to attend the library's reading group and all the community events that are running for families, but I can't do it all. I sometimes find the more we do, the "bittier" everything becomes. We get a little bit of this done, and a little bit of that, but we never see anything through to completion.

During phases whenever I have written books in the past, I did it as if someone was holding a gun to my head and telling me to hurry up, or else. I would churn out book after book, never spending much time on promoting them. I felt like I was on a high-speed setting on a treadmill and there was no emergency stop button. Usually, during those times, my body would become its own stop button: getting sick so I had no choice but to stop. Even whenever I was sick, there were times that I made myself keep writing, even if it was the last thing on Earth I wanted to do. Who was I trying to impress? Who was I trying to prove myself to? The only person that suffered was me. I would continuously burn myself out and to no avail. I would fire off hundreds of letters to literary agents, composing new synopses for every book I was trying to get published, and I'd be left feeling obliterated whenever I heard nothing back, got a rejection, or whenever I just needed to go to bed, and I wouldn't allow myself to do it. I sometimes reflect on those periods and think "would life have been any different today if I hadn't done any of that?" Maybe it's better to put more time into a slower developing writing project than to burn it all up, firing out books in all directions. My book-producing behaviour was almost a form of self-harm, and then whenever the books didn't succeed in the way I'd hoped they would, I'd use them as material to flog myself with.

I didn't know why I was doing it to myself, but it felt like I was scared of stopping because it might give me too much time to really look at my life, and then I might fall into despair.

I have begun to realise whenever you stop running, you are forced to look at your life, but it doesn't have to be in a self-critical way; it can be in a "how can I be better?" way. Faster isn't better and no one will give you a medal for rushing through life, doing as much as you possibly can and not attending to your own needs. No one wants to know someone like that either. They make them feel like they aren't doing enough themselves, and thus, the cycle continues. Maybe we can stop the cycle through our own actions. Whenever you feel compelled to achieve – instead you can put your feet up in the garden with a good book, or if reading doesn't appeal to you, just watch the sky, the comings and goings of birds and the changes in seasonal plants and feel a sense of completion in the little things you're allowed to do, if only you let yourself.

Chapter Seven

During my years of constantly being on the run, both from myself and from my home, I barely had time to do any housework. I always covered the basics, but clutter quickly accumulated. When you're out all the time, it's easy to accumulate lots of stuff, whether it's bought or gifted to you. You are just exposed to so much more of it because it's looking you in the face at every turn. Even going to the museum was a trip during which I had to impose rules around shopping. The museum itself is free to visit, but the café and the gift shop seem to require you to get out your bank card if you dare to set foot in them. I don't know who is responsible for curating the collections of goods on display in the Ulster Museum gift shop, but they're doing their job well. Every item in it, whether for children or adults, tempts me to pick it up. There are so many items for sale that provide gifts beyond the initial purchase. You can pick up books on arts and crafts and broadening your knowledge of a multitude of interesting topics. You can buy craft kits and temptingly presented boxes of high-quality pencils that can only be sharpened with their own specific sharpener that also happens to be on sale on their shelf. The arrangement of the items makes for easy purchasing; you don't have to run here and there looking for the separate components for one craft project; they are all conveniently located on the same surface. The prices are hiked up too. There have been times whenever I have googled books in the gift shop and found them for half the price online, but there is something charming about finding the physical object on a shop shelf. You don't have to wait for it, you just carry it to the till and you're greeted by a smiling shop assistant that offers to wrap it for you, like a little gift to yourself. I quickly had to implement a ban. You could spend hundreds in a minute if you let yourself do it. Following that, you can find a nook in the café and get yourself a pot of tea and some sweet treats. You don't have to take more than a handful, or rather, foot-ful of steps before coming across the next purchasing opportunity.

I have got much better at putting limits in place whenever we are out, in terms of allowed purchases. If I decide I won't make a single purchase before I enter a store, I keep that promise to myself. But being out all the time subjects you to a level of intensive marketing that you aren't as susceptible to at home. You can choose to keep your eyes away from the adverts placed on every social channel and every screen. It might take a little will to do it, but if you put your phone away and turn the TV off, peace is yours. In the last year, I've realised that I don't need to hear the constant noise of aggressive marketing. I can choose to remove myself from it by being more of a homebird. I'm not a homebody at heart; I love to travel and adventure, and I love novelty, but sometimes, for the sake of our finances and for our sanity, we need to hunker down and impose a period of hibernation for ourselves.

When it comes to housework, it makes life simpler too. I'm not someone that enjoys cleaning, but I enjoy the results of having done it. Whenever you spend your life running around, home feels like a billet. It doesn't feel like it encases you in its comforting warmth and it feels like it loses some of its essence of cosiness, because things aren't attended to. Purchases pile up on kitchen counters and they don't get put away. Whenever I am at home, I am less stressed because I attend to all the tasks that are demanding to be done. I can't turn a blind eye to them whenever they are staring me in the face day and night. I get round to decluttering and organising, and I want to make every area of my home more accessible to myself so life can feel easier. I have always been a bit of a natural hoarder but being at home forces me to confront my clutter and do something about it. To me, some clutter is homely. I don't want to live in a starkly minimalist space with no personality. I just want my home to be a place of comfort and not a place of stress; there is enough of that in the outside world. I didn't prioritise my home in recent years because I spent so little time in it. I was living like a transient in a way. It didn't help before we moved house that our house was in such a terrible state. I've always thought a little cleaning and dressing up goes a long way, but I didn't feel there was much I could do with the home we had. It's hard to

The Year I Stopped Running

cover up wallpaper that's hanging off the walls because of the dampness of the plaster behind it. It could have been redecorated daily and the same would have occurred each time because of the structural issues. The landlord refused to attend to them and that depressed me. I didn't want to return to the stench of damp and the appalling aesthetic of the place, but equally, I couldn't face moving again. I'd done it so many times in my adult life. Whenever my marriage broke down, I moved house five times in two years. I just wanted to feel settled, but I didn't know how to achieve that. Since I have bipolar disorder, the more I was out and the more stimulated I was by my external environment, the more "highs" I experienced that fed into the pattern of being on the run.

Moving into our new house put the brakes on, very abruptly. It removed us from our central location. It wasn't far away from the things we knew but it was far enough removed to inhibit the constant outings. We could no longer wander around the corner and into a selection of tempting cafes, or for a charity shop spree, or hop on a bus in seconds and get into town. Everything took a little longer. I still haven't found a local coffee shop I like as much as my beloved Café Nero, and that has ended up being a good thing because I figured out how to make the best coffee myself. I always thought coffee shop coffee couldn't be beaten, but my homemade lattes make café lattes taste disappointing these days. I still love a treat in Café Nero, but it has become a weekly or monthly one rather than a daily one. I have broken a habit that was hurting my finances, but also my sense of satisfaction. It's hard to truly appreciate something you do every single day. Even if it is something pleasant, it becomes monotonous when it turns into a daily expectation.

The area we live in has a completely different feel to it. It doesn't feel like it's in the middle of a bustling city environment. It's an incredibly quiet street with the houses spaced far apart. You could get dressed in front of the window and the neighbour opposite wouldn't even be able to see. (Not that I do that, but if I wanted to, I could!) In our last street, the houses were crammed together: semi-detached but with the spacing of a row of terraces. We each had a small back yard, and it felt like we were living on top of each other. There was a real sense of community, but there is a downside to that too. You could overhear every conversation in the street as people passed your house and there was no feeling of real privacy there.

I used to visit a house close to the one we live in now. It belonged to a friend, and I was always quietly envious of her sprawling garden. Now we have one of our own. It's a lot of work but I'm grateful for it. It takes time to maintain. I have to keep up with regularly cutting the grass and weeding and trimming hedges, but it gives me a focus that makes it feel like I am getting out of the house but without the feeling of rushing around, wasting time and petrol. I can see the fruits of my efforts, and there is satisfaction to be found in that. I like the imperfection of the gardens too. I like that the previous owner made their imprint on them. They were obviously a gardener, and we benefit from the beautiful plants they decided to acquire. The hydrangea bush thrives and produces sky blue flowers, just like I always dreamed of, and I don't have to do anything to it, other than the annual deadheading of the flowers. We have a redcurrant bush in the back corner of the back garden and my kids love to pick and eat them. It reminds me of my own childhood home where we had redcurrants that grew in abundance in the summer. I even took the time to pick them this year and to make some redcurrant jam and redcurrant gin. I learned just how much fruit it takes to make jam; something that I wasn't fully aware of or appreciative of until I did it myself. Taking the time to do things slowly by hand makes you gain an appreciation for the labour and love involved in creating things, and I love to use up the things that our garden naturally produces. Similarly, we live right beside an urban walkway. I didn't even realise until after we had moved in that there was a little shortcut from our street onto it. It feels like walking in a forest, and it only takes a minute to reach it. In the summer, there are so many blackberries growing on it that my kids and I can go blackberry picking and we don't even make a dent in the amount of them growing there. My dog even likes to sample them. There is something nostalgic and heartwarming about bringing a container and filling it with handpicked fruit. You could pay quite a bit of money to buy some pre-packaged ones in the shop, but we have them at our disposal for free. I have developed a feeling of gratitude since moving here and slowing down that I didn't have time to adequately experience in our last abode. I always made the best I could out of the little yard we had. I planted some flowers, even

The Year I Stopped Running

though I am terrible at keeping plants alive. When our wooden table and chairs started to fade, I painted them a sunshine yellow and we spent sunny days sitting in the garden, playing simple childhood games and having barbeques. Lockdown made us do that even more, but once it ended, we fell into running around again.

I often stop to ask myself why we don't get sick as often since moving house. Part of me attributes it to the damp that existed there, but another part of me puts it down to the fact we don't race around in the same way. Whenever you are out all the time, constantly putting yourself into busy social situations, you are fighting against the need for rest that your body has. I never allowed us to hit pause until we were struck down with sickness, and I'd always realise too late that we needed to have a rest. Sometimes I was so reluctant to slow down that I'd fight through sickness, telling myself if I just kept driving myself forwards, I'd will myself back to wellness.

Whenever I was little, my family were good at hibernation. We didn't run around all the time, wearing ourselves out. We spent a huge amount of time in our home, and I liked being there. It was only in those moments of boredom and slowness that my sister and I came up with the best games and utilised our creativity. Had we been out, running around all the time, I don't think I would have developed my creative instincts to the extent I did. I can remember spending hours sitting on my bed reading my way through every available library book. I read and reread so many that I exhausted the supply of children's books and had to move on to the adults' section. I devoured Agatha Christie mysteries and then I moved onto the classics, reading Jane Eyre around the age of ten and loving every second of it. I could appreciate the slow development of a plot and the atmosphere of a book. I wasn't just speed-reading so I could get something else done. I was immersed in reading to an extent I thought was impossible to recreate in adulthood. But it can be done. I have read over sixty books in the last year – almost all of them borrowed rather than bought - from the library around the corner from our house. My kids get as excited about our library outings as I do, and they love coming home with a bag so filled with books that the straps of our bag are strained. We practically need a wheelbarrow to carry them all home. I still love to curl up with some Agatha Christie on a frosty Winter's night, positioned cosily next to the Christmas tree, but my main genres are literary fiction and nonfiction now. Things change but our intrinsic loves from childhood often remain.

If I were to catalogue my favourite things to do as a child, very few of them would involve spending money. I didn't have the money to spend at the time anyway, so we had to be creative and focus on the meaningful over the costly. I had a metal teddy bear piggy bank in which I carefully kept the rare pound coin given to me by a grandparent and I saved them up. I don't remember spending my small collection; just counting them and keeping them safe in that sturdy tin. I'm sure it's still lurking somewhere in my parents' roof-space, probably with some pennies still left in it. I don't remember ever going out to spend money. I don't remember being promised shopping trips and expenditures. I do remember accompanying my mum and my granny into the city centre while they shopped, but most of it was window shopping. Of all those trips into town, I most remember going into a gift shop and my mum buying me a bottle of vivid green nail polish. I felt extremely wealthy whenever she did that. I treasured it and used it sparingly, trying to extend its life for as long as I possibly could. My point in writing all of this is to express that the rarity of that treat made me appreciate it so much more. When we are treating ourselves left, right and centre, it's hard to even keep track of what we have acquired. I can still remember the look of that bottle of nail polish as if I held it in my hand mere moments ago. If it had been a weekly event, I don't think I would have remembered the items as clearly. It helped that green was and still is my favourite colour. It made it even more special. I still adore green. I love looking at the green trees, plush carpets of green summer grass, a green Christmas tree, real or artificial, they are both equally green to me. We use the same one every year and it has served us well for nearly a decade. I never feel the need to run out and get a new one or to give myself the bother of acquiring a real fir tree. It feels like too much work whenever I already have everything I need right here. That was the view I started to take towards life on the whole. Why give myself the work and the exhaustion of running around whenever everything I needed was in my own home and local area?

The Year I Stopped Running

Whenever I was growing up, we lived in a small village of one thousand residents. Whenever I was little, we had one car that my dad took to work with him. I remember neighbours sharing lifts sometimes and going everywhere on foot. We often cut through a local graveyard to shorten our walk into the village. Those moments stand out to me as extremely special. Sometimes the simplest things make the deepest imprints on our subconsciouses. Walking on our local Greenway gives me the same feeling. Sometimes it's the most mundane thing that becomes our safest and most comforting habit. I hope my children will remember our daily walk with the dog, stopping off at the playground for a few minutes before turning back. My kids look forward to the familiar faces we pass whenever we are walking our dog. He has made doggy friends he gets excited to see and we have long conversations with some of their owners. It brightens our day sharing a few words with a stranger, even if it's just an exchange about the weather. I used to bemoan small talk, labelling it meaningless, but I've learnt it isn't. It isn't about the words said, it's about the exchange of positivity and the fact that you are building community whenever you do it. However reclusive you consider yourself to be, on some level, that is very important, and it is something that has died out in recent years. We have fallen into the habit of living very isolated existences, covering it up with our phone usage and apparent attempts at "contact," all the while failing to make real contact with a single person. It is a sad state for society to be in, if we stop to really think about it.

Making those small connections with people that you've never met but with whom you coexist in a pleasant society is worth more than all the money in the world.

Keelan LaForge

Chapter Eight

Whenever I stopped running around and limited our activities, I rediscovered a love for swimming. I have always been a competent swimmer, but I never considered it to be a real talent of mine. I still don't, but I absolutely love going swimming. Admittedly, it gets harder to be as disciplined about going with the arrival of the Winter months, but I'm always glad I did once I get into the pool. The pool we go to claims to keep its temperature very low for the water polo that I see being played there once every few months, so it is always an act of bravery taking the first step in. I used to think I wanted to go sea swimming, to the point that I even looked into getting wetsuits and almost bought them for myself and the kids. I'm so glad I didn't run with that impulse then. Dipping a toe in the freezing indoor pool is about as much as I can handle. I like a challenge, but a dip in the ice-cold sea sounds a step too far and I still haven't done it. Instead, I look on in awe as people run, clad in nothing but a swimsuit, shrieking as their bodies hit the just above freezing temperatures of the Irish sea. Had we kept moving at the pace we were, I don't think we would have made time to get into swimming. I knew I wanted the girls to take lessons, primarily for safety reasons but I never foresaw myself getting into the pool with them. I planned to drop them at the poolside and let the instructors do their job, watching from the café window as I waited with the other parents, but I quickly felt drawn to get into the water too. Watching them taking to swimming like little fish made me want to improve my own swimming, and to just get immersed in the water and switch off from the rest of life. I quickly realised that whenever I'm in the water, everything else ceases to exist. My mind goes quiet, and I feel nothing but the water on my body and the strokes I take to get from one end of the pool to the other. I started off going swimming whenever my kids were at their lesson, and now I go with them and whenever they are in school. It resets something in me, and I have always loved being in water. Swimming isn't a costly activity – at least not in the pool we go to. If I divide the monthly fee up cost per visit, it's only a couple of pounds per time and the benefits are immeasurable. I recently discovered that our monthly payment covers another pool in our area, so we have started to go there too. It has a spa we can visit that happens to be included in the price, so my partner and I go on his days off work whenever the kids are in school. Going for a swim, followed by a steam room, sauna and a lie down on the heated tile beds might be one of the most relaxing things I have ever done, and it doesn't cost us an extra penny.

Simplifying and stripping back our lives has opened up time to devote to more fulfilling hobbies. I began to realise how much I love being active. I have never been a gym lover, even in the days whenever I used to force myself to go. It's too hot and sweaty, like being trapped inside an athlete's old shoe. But water and fresh air are a different matter entirely. I love going for a brisk walk with my dog, even in winter – maybe even more so. I love the freshness of the air as it hits your lungs with its clarifying coldness. Mentally, I process so much information while I walk. It helps me to get in touch with what is really important to me values-wise. I have always loved practising yoga at home too. I used to attend classes whenever I was younger, but I never practised it between classes. I got a free yoga mat a couple of years ago and since having more time in the house, I have created the habit of practising it almost daily. The calm and flexibility yoga gives me are invaluable, and as I get further into my thirties, I notice the physical benefits so much more than I did whenever I was younger.

Being active in the ways that I actually find enjoyable has made exercise so much more appealing to me and having the extra downtime to devote to what I really want to do has been an enormous gift this year.

The Year I Stopped Running

Chapter Nine

I used to have an addiction to buying dresses. Not even clothes in general: just dresses. I was always hunting for the next dress. Most of them were vintage or second hand, but it was still problematic. I'd buy so many I couldn't even close my wardrobe. It would sit permanently ajar with fabric bulging out of the sides of it. It was off-putting. It made me not want to decide what to wear in the morning. The beauty of a single dress was lost in the masses of material. Whatever made one stand out as singularly unique in the shop wasn't visible whenever it was just another dress forced into my perpetually overfilled wardrobe. I considered it to be a hobby, but what was I really buying? I was buying a momentary appreciation for something and losing that appreciation for it as soon as I brought it home. I thought owning something was the same as appreciating it. I felt a sense of fear that if I didn't buy a dress I liked, someone else would. But why did that cause me fear? I have learnt that there will always be another dress. No matter how many beautiful ones you find, there will always be another one to love. You can never possess them all. I have seen clothing that I have loved but immediately written off as an impossible purchase due to its price tag. I never considered buying a dress over sixty pounds because I knew that would cull my dress-buying habit. If I did that, I would have to cease buying any more. I couldn't justify buying more if I blew all my money on one thing. But in hindsight, maybe that would have been better. Whenever you buy in an impulsive way, rather than saving for and admiring one item from afar before investing real money in it, it all just blends together. You never reach a level of satisfaction or real enjoyment of that one item. You're always seeking the next one. As soon as you're finished shopping for one, you start shopping for another. It becomes part of a collection rather than something singularly valued. Whenever I was making purchases like that, I never had any money left at the end of the month. It drained away in small amounts, so I didn't see the full picture of my purchases. Maybe if I had made one considered purchase instead, the overall effect on my finances would have been less damaging.

Whenever we moved house, I had to start limiting my dress purchases. They became a less often extravagance rather than a monthly or even weekly habit. I started to work on decreasing the number of items in my wardrobe, rather than cramming more and more in. Whenever you force more clothing into a space that can't accommodate it, all that happens is it becomes impossible to see what's inside, and you end up having to iron everything again because it all becomes so creased. My wardrobe was a source of stress to me, so I started selling dresses on Vinted. They were incredibly quick to list and once I sold one, the momentum built, and I wanted to declutter more and more. Whatever momentary sadness I felt at packing the dresses up was gone as soon as I dropped off the parcel. I forgot them as soon as they set off on their way to someone else's wardrobe. There were dresses that I really liked, but that I sold because I couldn't accommodate them, and I never think of them now. I mustn't have loved them because I was able to sell them, and not owning them has only improved my quality of life. I can see what's in my wardrobe now and I can get dressed with ease. I can still express myself artistically through my clothing and by pairing items differently. If anything, having less clothing has made me more creative with the clothing I do have. I experiment with outfit combinations I wouldn't have had the time to think of otherwise. There was a time whenever I could have worn a different dress every day for months and I wouldn't have got the chance to develop a real attachment or fondness for any piece of clothing. I think the love for our clothing grows whenever we wear something more and more and it moulds to fit our individual bodies. It becomes a reflection of our personalities, and it gains character with each wear.

Recently, I have been learning more and more about clothing repair and the techniques used to do it. There are countless ways to fix your clothing and make it more unique. A tear doesn't have to mean the end of a garment's life. It can be the beginning of it becoming something completely individual

The Year I Stopped Running

that expresses your personality. I still haven't mastered patching techniques, but I am working on it. My partner's T-shirt had huge tears in it, so I recently patched it with some leftover material I had from a dress I'm working on upcycling into a skirt. The fabric happened to go very well with the secondary colours in the T-shirt and it added something to the T-shirt that made it different. I also added some pockets to his hoody this week. It has an image that covers the front of it, so I added them to the back instead. They are so big they are more like extra bags than pockets. It required a bit of experimentation on my part because I have never added pockets to his clothing before, but he ordered some fabric with a print he liked on it, and it made it look unique. I love the idea of making my own clothes, but the reality of it is different than my imagined version. It causes me huge amounts of stress, but repairing clothing is something entirely different and much more enjoyable.

Whenever I think back to my teenage years, my wardrobe was much more condensed. I was just beginning to discover my own personal style and I did it using a select number of items. At that time, I loved to layer pieces to create my desired look like I do now. I wore two tops to death and changed my look by adding different pairs of colourful tights under my ripped jeans. I had an army jacket on which I changed the buttons from plain ones to butterflies and added some patches to. I had a pair of shoes my friends got me for my birthday, and I wore them until they literally fell apart. There is something much more satisfying about really wearing items you love compared with hoarding unworn clothes in an overstuffed wardrobe. I felt richer with a select number of items I genuinely loved rather than a large collection of underappreciated pieces. I had a favourite wrap around cardigan I acquired from my sister that could be tied in different ways. It got ruined by someone scorching it with a cigarette in a nightclub and I still feel a little disappointed when I remember that happening. That attitude of my teenage years stemmed from having little money to spend on clothing, but it meant I treasured the things I had.

I wanted to cultivate that attitude again, and after moving house, I had less disposable income to spend on clothes, so I worked on making my wardrobe something I truly loved. I sold a lot of unworn pieces on Vinted and passed them on to loving homes where they'd hopefully be more often worn and appreciated. I felt an airiness returning to my wardrobe. I had felt envious whenever I looked at the pared back wardrobes of minimalists online. I wanted room for colourful creativity and self-expression in my own wardrobe but with fewer loved pieces to work with. I wanted to be able to open and close my wardrobe with ease, so it could serve its intended purpose. So much of what we have nowadays is overfilled and overstuffed. It makes life more difficult for us and it makes the simplest decisions exhausting and time consuming. Now, whenever I slide open my wardrobe, I feel good knowing that I am happy to wear its full contents and that I have decluttered the pieces that made me less comfortable or that didn't suit me, colour, size or style-wise.

Clothing or otherwise, I realised that the more I buy, the more decision fatigue I get after the purchase. I have to find a home for each item, I have to clean it and clean around it and I have to remember to use it. It made me want to be more considered about the items I purchased to avoid that feeling of overwhelm creeping back in.

Why is excess so celebrated in our society whenever it brings us nothing but stress and financial problems? We see one person with something, and we immediately believe it to be a need, but is it? If you strip everything back to survival terms, what do we really need to survive? I wanted to adopt that view more and more and make my home a sanctuary by getting rid of the things I didn't use. The need to constantly cull isn't a peaceful feeling, and it makes our home feel less homely. I don't mind slowly weeding out what we don't use but whenever I'm overwhelmed with the number of items, it doesn't make for a pleasant living environment, and I feel emotionally overwhelmed too. It doesn't matter if it's an overfilled wardrobe or an overfilled pantry; if a space is cluttered, I can't cope with it, so I look at it less and less, hiding it away from sight like a secret I don't want to face up to.

I want my clothing to be well thought out and to always fit with my tastes. That is one reason why I've had to cut back so much on my charity shop visits. Thrifting has been a hobby of mine since charity shops first existed in

The Year I Stopped Running

Northern Ireland. I loved finding quirky pieces that spoke of my personal style, and I loved going through clothing rails, never knowing if I would find something and being surprised by the perfect find. But my visits became more and more frequent. There was a time whenever I was coming home almost every day with a bag in hand, and I thought I loved every piece, but they just got lost in the clutter once they came into the house. There were items I realised I didn't like beyond the initial moment of interest in them. I might have liked the idea of them or that shiny first glimpse of them, but it wasn't an enduring kind of love. I wanted to give them away again as soon as I got home. I think it's a positive that I didn't love fast fashion, and I was at least giving a home to second hand items, but if you aren't going to use something, it's as much use sitting in your house as it would be sitting in landfill. It's just taking up space on Earth without doing anything. I knew that my charity shopping was becoming an addiction whenever I couldn't stay away from the shops and I couldn't resist the urge to buy something; anything. It became like an item on a never-ending to-do list. You can be a consumer of charity shop items too. It mightn't be creating as many environmental problems whenever you purchase from them, but it still leads to clutter and financial ruin if you do it enough. Instead of buying one higher priced dress, I'd find myself buying ten for the same price. Ten new items on a regular basis becomes impossible to accommodate in your home. If you buy one new item you love, you're going to feel much more excited about it and wear it to death. But if you buy ten cheap versions, you're going to view them as less valuable and be less inclined to use them, in my experience. I thought I was rescuing items from going to landfill, but really, I was just hoarding them, and it wasn't good for my mental health, nor was it good for my physical space. I found myself with shelves frequently emptying their contents onto my head, I struggled to fit anything into the containers we had. It felt like cupboards had to serve multiple purposes whenever they couldn't even hold their intended contents. A kitchen cupboard would become a craft cupboard and a tool cupboard and a holiday supply cupboard; all of it becoming one cluttered mess.

I realised that if I put myself in shopping situations, I would always find something new to buy, because there is always something new. I knew I needed to say no to myself more often, and that meant banning myself from regularly visiting charity shops. I tried to change my mindset from "what can I buy?" to "what can I stop buying?" I began to notice the number of possessions in our household declining and I felt lighter in every way.

Charity shops can be a good way to find bargains if they are used less frequently or in a conscious way. But if they are just an excuse to pile as much as we can fit into our baskets, it ruins the joy of finding a hidden treasure - which reminds me of a Kurt Cobain quote I heard once. He said that going in and being able to buy the whole store wasn't the same as finding a little treasure whenever he had no money and not knowing for sure if he could afford it or not. Things only feel special whenever we can't do them all the time.

I realised the same could be applied to everything in life. I started to reconsider my actions in life and to see what I could afford to cut (and often what I couldn't afford to not cut!) I knew I had a coffee shop addiction. It provided me with the perfect environment in which to write and to enjoy my free time whenever the kids were in school. The fact that my favourite coffee shop happened to be located two blocks from their school made it too convenient. Before we moved house, I could walk there in under five minutes too. I ran through my bank statements, and it hit me just how much my little habit was a big problem. The payments to the coffee shop featured more regularly than any other payment. I felt like everything in the world would only be OK if I just got myself that overpriced cup of coffee. It had become like a new coping mechanism for life. I'd replaced smoking cigarettes with buying coffee instead. The thing was, I had all the coffee making equipment I needed to recreate my beloved lattes at home, but I came up with excuses not to do it. If we happened to stay at home at the weekend or if we were sick, I would make my own lattes, but it was the exception rather than the rule. I decided to make life a bit easier for my lazy self and I got an electric milk frother. I knew if I could pour the milk in and just press a button, I'd be much more likely to do it often than if had to use the manual one with the plunger that I already had. Getting the electric frother was transformative. I used to make lattes for guests, and I had to use the plunger one cup at a time

The Year I Stopped Running

since that was all the milk it would hold. Now I can quickly make the milk as the coffee simmers and it's much more streamlined and easier. Sometimes appliances are worth investing in if they help you change your habits overall. It mightn't be a necessary purchase for a lot of people, but as a picky coffee drinker, it has completely changed my coffee drinking routine. I rarely go to coffee shops anymore. I reserve them for meetings with a friend or dates when my boyfriend is off work. I don't just go every time I'm trying to kill half an hour or because I feel like it. I have created my own café atmosphere at home, and it has become preferable to the ambience I find in cafés. Whenever I enter them now, the music often irritates me or the volume of the voices around me are harder to tune out. I've got used to my cosy and quiet kitchen café.

At this phase of motherhood, I find that I am spending more and more of my time providing a taxi service for my kids. Whenever they needed to be dropped somewhere, I used to always squeeze in a coffee shop latte before I had to pick them up again. Now, I plan ahead in small ways to discourage myself from doing that, and I have realised that I quite like hanging out in my car. I can read and watch videos or just people watch through the windscreen. I'm lucky enough to have heating and all the music I would choose to listen to if I had any say in my favourite café's playlist. There's something almost romantic about sitting in the car whenever the winter nights are closing in. You find yourself sitting in darkness, thankful for the light and warmth of the car, the cup holder that sits so conveniently beside you, the view from the windows of cosy lamplight from the surrounding houses, the passing dogs going for their daily walks, the Christmas lights whenever they appear. The short days are a novelty at the moment in the same way that the long ones will be whenever we reach the Spring. I love the change in the seasons, and I notice them in more detail than I ever have before. Maybe it is because whenever you slow down your pace in life, you have time to notice the tiniest traces of beauty that you overlooked beforehand.

Keelan LaForge

Chapter Ten

The more time I spend in my house, the more time I put into cooking. Cooking nourishes the spirit just as much as the stomach. I have always enjoyed cooking from scratch, with oven food featuring very little in our diet. I like to stick a premade pizza in the oven as much as the busiest of workers, but I prefer making my own with my hands and seeing the raw ingredients become pliable dough and then a crisp and cushiony crust. There is something much more rewarding about knowing you made it yourself, not to mention the fact that the taste of homemade pizza is far superior to the kind in plastic packaging. But I'm not against using frozen pizza either. If I have less time, I'm happy with a shop bought pizza, but I like to be immersed in the sensory experience of working with the dough. I like the Italian scents that fill the kitchen whenever I make my own pizza sauce too.

With more time for the slower things in life, I love to make my own bread too. The loaves mightn't always be bakery-level goods, but I love a piece of homemade toast with a thick layer of peanut butter and some complimentary jam. Whenever I make bread, I can use up the scraps in other recipes. It makes the most delicious French toast and croutons, and I recently transformed a baguette into garlic bread. It makes the best breadcrumbs for meatballs and macaroni cheese topping too. Convenience is an amazing thing to have with a quick tap of our bank cards, but sometimes you can't beat the homemade version.

I have always loved watching videos and reading books about slow, mindful living. I often envied other people's ability to move at a slower pace through life. I felt like I was always driving myself, even though I wasn't working in the conventional sense. Since everything went awry with my health after I finished my university degree and I didn't end up in the secure job I'd hoped I would, I felt like a failure. I looked around at my peers and I felt less rounded than them. From afar, they seemed to be doing so much with their lives, and I wished I could achieve a tenth of what others did. Maybe that was what led to me publishing books. I'd always been a reader, and I had toyed with the idea of writing my own stories, but the idea wasn't cemented until after I thought I had failed at life. Writing wasn't about money or acclaim or any other seemingly unachievable goals; it was a release for me, and it gave me a sense of purpose. I felt like I had a job whenever I did it. I could set daily writing goals for myself, and I made it my job. I had a daily wordcount set: two thousand words and I told myself that I had to hit it no matter what. I didn't allow myself to ever take breaks because I knew that breaks equalled not finishing a book. I wanted to get my books out there as quickly as possible even if I nearly killed myself doing it. I didn't allow the quality to suffer either. I put myself through rigorous proofreading and editing, not realising that the closer you are to a piece of work, the less easily you can detect its flaws. I was exhausted, and I didn't have a critical boss standing over me, but I acted like I did. I did it to myself. Had I had someone standing over me with a cane, I wouldn't have felt any more pressure to perform. I was trying to justify my existence through my writing. Our society is very keen on making us feel inadequate if we aren't hitting certain milestones. Not having a well-paid job, a home of our own, a car, a partner, kids, disposable income, social events, a wide circle of friends; the list is endless and its bullet points endlessly exhausting to enumerate.

But I have never wanted to bend to meet societal expectations, so why was I driving myself so much? The busier I was, the less time I had to think and the more I produced, the more I felt a sense of value in myself and my existence, even though it has nothing to do with that. I felt that my worth was measured in what I produced rather than in who I was. It was a recipe for a breakdown. I churned out book after book, not allowing myself a day's rest between finishing one and starting another. It became like a form of self-punishment. Whenever I started, I enjoyed writing, but about thirty books later, I realised I was no longer enjoying it. I had sucked the joy out of it by making it into a duty. Even whenever I was physically ill with the flu or something equally flooring, I made myself continue. I wrote as I was slumped

The Year I Stopped Running

over my computer, indescribably wrung out. My words probably began to convey that too. I was losing the passion for it and my reviews began to confirm that to me too. People's responses to my writing became flatter and I seemed to attract hypercritical reviewers. It felt like they were picking apart the last seams of confidence I had in my writing, so I decided to quit.

I let my writing fall to the wayside, and I started to use my laptop so infrequently that it was never charged, sitting in the corner of the room, like a reminder of an abandoned dream. That made me feel guilty now and again: that I had dropped it as ruthlessly as I had. I just couldn't face doing it anymore.

I had finally hit burnout: the one that several people had predicted without saying those direct words. Their advice usually came in the form of statements like, "how do you produce so many books?" but I could read between the lines. They looked nonplussed whenever they asked it, but I knew the truth of it. I could produce so many books because I was sacrificing my wellbeing to do it. Writing: the thing I loved to do, had become a form of self-punishment and it had taken all the fun out of it. I had lost my love for it. I knew I needed to stop, and I wasn't sure if it would be forever, but I knew I needed to stop for a significant amount of time.

Whenever I was writing every day, I didn't have as much time for other things. Even though I had trained myself to tap out two thousand words in an hour, I felt spent after it. I didn't have time for other hobbies, and I felt drained without knowing the exact reason for it. Receiving a very negative review really affected me but it made me stop and rethink what I'd been doing. I realised I was wasting my words on the wrong audience, and I didn't know how to find the right audience, so I knew I needed to stop trying.

With less time spent on writing, I started to redirect that time into hobbies that didn't demand results from me. I realised that I felt fine without hitting my daily word count. I'd almost convinced myself I had to keep it up or my whole world would collapse. Maybe for a while, that was the case; it was the one thing holding me together through difficult times, but it had ceased to fulfil that purpose. I spent more time reading other people's work and absorbing inspiration from other people's art. I had more time to clean my house, cook and bake. I had more time to do activities with my kids without feeling the need to photograph and catalogue everything we did for the sake of my blog posts. I could do things slowly and really savour them. An important balancing act needs to take place between creating art and allowing yourself to enjoy your life, and I needed to quit writing for a while to learn how to do it.

Obviously, I am writing again (this book might be a bit of a giveaway!) but I am writing about a topic I want to share rather than out of a sense of obligation to my self-imposed writing schedule or impossible to sustain writing targets.

Chapter Eleven

I have been guilty of hoarding craft supplies in phases of my life. I have too many interests and too many desired hobbies I want to try out, but it can become overwhelming whenever you try to fit in too many at once. Just because you set something aside for a while, it doesn't mean you have to give it up entirely, but if you do, I'm trying to tell myself that's fine too. I have a cross-stitch sampler I still haven't finished because I'm not in the mood for it, and that's OK. I want to do other things at the moment, but it will be waiting for me in my craft box whenever I want to return to it. There is a difference between ridding yourself of things you will never use and getting rid of things you just don't want to use right now. I think decluttering has helped my stress levels, but I still have a long way to go with it. Sometimes you need to face up to the fact that you will never return to a hobby again and offloading it from your physical space and your mental to-do list feels like releasing yourself from the obligation of lugging around a heavy burden.

I have never been naturally skilled at the art of doing nothing. I used to overwork myself in school. I was always driven about doing my own homework, but I suffered from burn-out quite often. I had lots of clubs I attended in school. I always seemed to take on extra things to do. Whenever I graduated, I got sick, and I lost my sense of purpose. I was so disappointed in myself for not following the career route that I had predicted for myself. Instead, I ended up living a secluded existence back at home, which led to getting married, having children and then becoming a stay-at-home single mum. To me, that equalled failure. I filled every free moment with writing and creating. If I wasn't writing a book, I was blogging, or painting or submitting articles and stories to publications and competitions and getting sick and depressed again and again and again. It was a recipe for burnout that I'd come up with all by myself.

Whenever you are busy all the time and filling every waking moment with productivity, it becomes hard to switch off. It becomes a coping mechanism for living, and you get increasingly uncomfortable with the quiet moments whenever you have to face yourself. But to look after ourselves properly, we have to do that. It's funny how the thing I most dreaded (moving outside my area and to a quieter one) has ended up providing me with endless opportunities to slow down and take stock of what really matters. Whenever I lived in a more central location, I used to run around all the time, coming up with excuses to pop out to the shop and to the café every day. Now, I just have a library nearby and going there enriches us as a family. It stops us spending money and it provides us with such richness. I used to feel extremely uncomfortable with silence, filling it with music and background noise and constant distractions, but this year, I have finally settled into it. I still love to listen to a favourite album and to have a video running in the background to motivate me while I clean, but I'm comfortable in the silence too. I like staring at the stars in a quiet sky, watching the birds' silent movements from behind my window, noticing the sunrise and sunsets and listening to the calming sound of my dog snoring. I like to sit and look around me and feel grateful that my life is so good and that I am so easily pleased. I needed to stop running to realise that. Now I appreciate a leisurely dander instead. I see all the beautiful things along the way that used to be nothing but a blur when I had my running shoes on, and I didn't let myself stop long enough to have a proper look at life.

Printed in Great Britain
by Amazon